The House Next Door to Africa

DENIS HIRSON

The House Next Door to Africa

CARCANET

First published in Great Britain 1987 by
Carcanet Press Limited
208–212 Corn Exchange Buildings
Manchester M4 3BQ

Carcanet
198 Sixth Avenue
New York
New York 10013

First published by David Philip Publisher (Pty) Ltd,
South Africa, 1986
Copyright © Denis Hirson 1986, 1987

British Library Cataloguing in Publication Data
Hirson, Denis
    The House Next Door to Africa.
    I. Title
    823 [F]   PR9369.3.H5/

    ISBN 0-85635-720-0

The publisher acknowledges financial assistance
from the Arts Council of Great Britain

Printed in England by SRP Ltd, Exeter

For my parents and grandparents

The echo in heaven

When an echo rolls out on an errand it can't stop. On reaching its destination it can't stop. And it has great difficulty pausing in the middle. There seems no end to the work of an echo. It must always be returning, bending and condensing what came before.

Eventually, it is small enough to slip under the doors of its soundproof heaven, far from the falling branches, the risky walls, the bullets and the footsteps. Then it can stop shaking the air, and stoop down, and forget.

But sooner or later a god bursts out, or a lost soul starts pounding to be let in, or a band of angels arrives on a cloud. The doors slide open and the echo wakes up, restlessly wondering where it came from, and what all that noise is about outside.

I   Path

Great-grandmother Dvorah is obsessed with her bag, which is continually getting lost. Search parties have to be organised to find it. The bag is allegedly stuffed with cheques, but when it is found the cheques are missing. Whereupon Great-grandmother Dvorah accuses Martha, the black maid, of theft. So Martha manufactures false cheques, seals them in envelopes, and slips them secretly into the bag.

★

Great-grandmother Dvorah locks herself up in the toilet, in the belief that she is on the train back to Russia. She removes the key from the door, and soon forgets where she has put it. Grandpa Joe is obliged to climb through the high window overlooking the backyard, to retrieve her. She emerges exhausted, and must lie down.

★

She treats her daughter, Granny Lily, as a sister, and cannot make sense of Grandpa Joe's presence in the house. She comes to the conclusion that he must be a stranger in the village, one of those Russian boys who goes from one house to the next for his evening meals. But why then has he been eating at their table for weeks on end?

★

Great-grandmother Dvorah can't find her bag again. Everyone in the house is mobilised to hunt it down. Martha is suspect number one, and Great-grandmother Dvorah strides across the backyard to make a pogrom in her room. But the bag is nowhere to be found. By the end of the day, when Grandpa Joe returns home, there is a state of emergency. He opens the fridge door for a glass of iced water and finds the bag, cold and black, jammed between the bottles in the door.

★

In the evening, Great-grandmother Dvorah stands outside under the plane trees, waiting for Aunty Essie's smart blue Fiat to pull up and take her home. She picks on the first car which stops in the street, so convinced it is Essie's that she refuses to release her grip on the door handle. She is inspired with great strength on such occasions; only when reminded that she has left her bag full of cheques inside the house does she let go.

★

She confides to Granny Lily that the backyard is a dried-up river bed. 'Come down to the river with me,' she proposes, 'it's such a long time since we washed.'

6

Grandpa Joe can sit still for longer than anyone else I know, and he can do it without saying a single word. On the floor next to his floral olive-green easy chair there lies a pile of Popular Scientists and Reader's Digests. More often than not, his face is buried up to the eyes in pages.

I stand at the doorway, concentrating all my attention on his eyelids to see if they will bat. Or he might lift his nostrils out of the pages and give a small snort. This could mean that he has fallen asleep, but it could also mean that he is just waking up. Then his head drops down again, and it is difficult to tell one way or the other.

Grandpa Joe's chair is set in the bay window of the living room, between the giant fern and the little wooden dog that has hours in one eye and minutes in the other, and something wrong with its springs. Behind the easy chair, the daylight is contained in the chiffon curtains. Before it, on the glass-topped table that occupies most of the room, there is a pale slice of silver. Otherwise, the room has the bleakness of the bottom of a lagoon through which the smooth, indolent voices of Springbok Radio filter constantly.

An aroma of sweetmeats and sugary wine and playing cards escapes from the sideboard against the far wall. Various contemporary members of the family, most of them from the shoulders up and several of them twice or three times over, look on from the stone mantelpiece, from the sideboard, and from under the glass on the table, as the house subsides through the afternoon in an airtight hush.

Grandpa Joe always seems to know who is there. At least, when the telephone rings, he knows whether no one else will answer, and he knows when he can carry on dozing.

He stands four-square in the passage, braces crossed over his khaki shirt, a stubby man with short grey hair surrounding the gleam on his head, and a smell about him of the tinned blue mud he uses to get the grease out of his hands. He lifts the black bakelite receiver off the hook and delivers himself of the word 'Hello', managing to clip it into a single syllable. He listens an instant, then leaves the receiver dangling over the lotuses on the passage carpet and goes off to the back door. 'Martha!'

Martha, Grandpa Joe's sworn enemy, appears. She is a bulky woman, with wary eyes bulging a little out of a stern, speckled face. When she picks up the receiver her features gradually soften and stir into life. Her Zulu comes out volubly, heavily humming, and for a very long time. Meanwhile, Grandpa Joe returns to the refuge and strength of his easy chair, where he sits so still in the gathering gloom that no one would guess he had ever moved.

★

It happens to him just this once, when he flies over to his Promised Land. He gets only butter beans to eat because there is a war on, but he doesn't mind. After all, it is his war. And then the policemen go around calling everyone 'Yankele'. Just this once he doesn't feel like a stranger. His cheek muscles hurt with all the smiling.

He goes for a walk up a sand road, passing a donkey-drawn ice-cart on its way down. Between the blotches of water in the sand he does a little slalom, then interrupts himself to

8

.

glance shyly about.

Houses line one side of the road. The clumps of grass in the garden have not yet knitted together, low bougainvillaea and plumbago bushes hug the cement and wood and corrugated iron of the walls. The flowers are filled with fire. His skin, blanched as root under an upturned rock and unprotected despite all warning, has already begun to suffer.

Sweating, he reaches the top of the road and looks around at the houses, the knotted, snapped gold of scrub opposite. Further down, the dark gloss of the orange grove promises coolness.

He is still standing there when a policeman, just off duty and wanting to be home for the hourly news broadcast, pauses to address him: 'Hey, Yankele, what's the time?'

It happens to him just this once, as he stands there at the top of the road, watching the policeman dwindle out of sight. His breaths lengthen slowly and bring sighs through his body. His mouth cakes up. His ribcage aches to open and release the weeping inside him, a bird with wet wings, Yankele: the bird of his own name.

Walls, fields, the orchard begin to bloat and sink and seethe in waves of light and shadow. He blinks, hard, but the warp won't go. The weeping stretches and trembles through him; the road is tugged from under his feet.

He finds himself on the hot sand. Sun-rays splinter in his eyes, there is a hammering in his head. Testing the firmness of the world he gets up, shakes out his sandals, dabs the

9

sweat from his face with a starched handkerchief. He then makes his uncertain way back down the burning road.

★

Across the yard stands Grandpa Joe's workshop, behind dirty purple bricks, under a peeling red roof. To one side there is the Goodmans' wall with its glinting fins of broken glass past which all balls are gone forever; there is also Mr Goodman's solid polished voice leading a second, tremulous voice, up and down the scales on the way to a barmitzvah. To the other side there is Martha's room with its reek of fermentation and drying meat.

In the obscurity of the workshop there are shelves loaded with bolts, washers, elements, castors, the aftermaths of toasters, hot-plates, irons, wirelesses, that engulf trays, boxes, bottles and the grey ghosts of bottles. From the rafters are strung giant springs and rolls and scribbles and shreds of metal and wire. And fleck by fleck everything diminishes into the rusty air, trailing a smell of burnt firecrackers and the space behind beds.

Grandpa Joe is somewhere in there, fixing things, and he must be called out to eat his chicken soup before he disappears entirely. I find him squinting down the shaft of a screwdriver in the drifts of rust. Behind him, two yellow horns of light come in at the window. Already he is much smaller than before. I say his name, but the air absorbs it. He is concentrating so hard that only the grooved head of the screw exists any more; all that is left of him are the furrows in his forehead, the grease-stains on his steady hands.

Granny Lily is standing in the driveway at the end of the daisy bed, watching the leaves drip. Willy the gardener has just passed through, alcohol on his breath and blood-vessels in his eyes, propelling a hosepipe before him and wetting everything in sight. The hosepipe is still writhing around the corner. The water brings fragrance from the flowers and the grass.

Next to Granny Lily is Grandpa Joe's electricity van, stolid and oblong and sleet grey on its four flat tyres. To her left is Grandpa Joe's head, immobile in the window.

She looks tired. Her cheeks are loose and pale with talcum dust, her shoulders are bunched up. The redness of her lips deepens at the corners and there is a dimple of shadow on her forehead. She could be standing in a boxing ring some time after everyone else had gone home. The air is full of old blows.

But the garden is splashed with sunlight, and it is for the sunlight that Granny Lily has prepared herself. Her shin-length dress is white with a navy-blue deer-hoof pattern; there is an unblemished ivory profile on her cameo brooch. Her gathered-leather handbag is white, as are the shoes from which emerge the tortoise-heads of her big toes.

The whiteness bounces daisy by daisy from her outfit to where I wait on the porch, peeling some more paint off the wall and working out the kind of shape it leaves behind.

We are going out. Aunty Essie should be arriving any minute now in her rattling Fiat with the running-boards and stalk-eyed headlamps, and we'll be off, wrapped in a stupor of permanent hair-wave lacquer, lipstick and filter-tipped fumes.

After that there will be as much grass as possible, ponds of slime lined with fat-headed jelly-tailed tadpoles waiting to be scooped up, candyfloss and sparkling toffee apples and thick, frothy strawberry milkshakes, while for some inexplicable reason Granny Lily and Aunty Essie stick to tea and scones.

With any luck there will be an elephant nonchalantly dropping dung, waiting for me to hand in my ticket and get on. The elephant saunters off, the sky begins to rock from side to side and trees sweep the clouds. Everyone screams blue murder and glee.

The elephant driver, in a bus-conductor uniform, has lifted his bottom out of the saddle to stick his nose into the elephant's ear, whispering soothing secrets while he digs his thin silver crowbar into its skull. There is a terrific trumpeting. The ground shudders open, swallowing all the cages in the zoo.

Then the clouds slow down. One by one the trees return, clinging tightly to the ground. It is time for me to be hoisted off, feeling dizzy and in urgent need of another milkshake.

Wherever we are, Granny Lily and Aunty Essie make for the nearest bench in the shade. Granny Lily, the shorter and stouter of the two, has arms that wobble when she walks and shoulders up to her neck. She says if you smoke cigarettes your bones shrink. They arrange themselves on the bench, take out their knitting, and conspire softly in a language that sounds like English, but turns into Yiddish if I come too close.

Granny Lily is standing at the end of the daisy bed, her legs planted slightly apart, her hair permed and nearly blue, her bag hooked to her hip, waiting. She looks down at her watch again. Aunty Essie should be arriving any minute now.

★

All the old ladies turn nervously this way and that, their black dresses flouncing into each other, falling past the knee-cap. Their black shoes lift and perch and shift and soon return to where they were.

Their wrinkles are all dabbed with Granny Lily's talcum powder, their lips are stuck together with Granny Lily's lipstick. They have all recently sat under the hot hives at the hair-dresser's, filed their nails, pushed down the cuticles to show the rising moons, and painted them red. Their arms are crinkled, their legs are each seamed together at the back.

They hang on to their black bags as if their lives depended on it, narrowly missing each other, closing in on each other like curtains. Somewhere behind them Granny Lily is dying; I must get past them to find her. But they pay no attention, they are so preoccupied, their glances flying without aim from their grim faces.

Somewhere behind them, on a floral olive-green sofa, Granny Lily is dying. My father is curled in deep sleep with his head on her lap. He is wearing his baggy grey trousers and glasses, his moustache goes placidly up and down.

13

Grandpa Joe, unusually refreshed and alert, is facing them from his easy chair under the giant fern. Just the other side of the fern, on the floor, lies a fat book with a glittering gold title; on it is a stranger with a narrow olive-skinned face, cross-legged, tall and poised as an arrow.

If they have noticed Granny Lily they don't show it. Her face is turned away from them, and does not move. The grey filaments of her hair pull in disorder from her scalp, burning with a light of their own. Her mouth is stretched open till the blood leaves her lips, but no word emerges. Her eyes drive blankly into the distance where some horror hardens them. Nothing and no one will divert them from their path.

★

The steam is everywhere. It lounges around the floor under the ceiling, under tables and chairs, puffs itself up and eventually swallows the old fridge, which goes on croaking indistinctly. Steam escapes the lips of the tall, bubbling pots and burps into the steam that preceded it, rolls over tins of teigelach and beigelach and kiggelach and climbs the walls till they sweat with exhaustion.

Through the steam comes a procession of hands bearing orange rubber seals, portholes of cellophane paper, little Tate and Lyle men riding their sugar packets, a pair of squeaky scales, newly boiled ball-jars whose mouths glitter and breathe still further steam. The hands glide disembodied, deftly, foreknowing, to and fro between the invisible pantry and the damp roses on the plastic table-top, where they are seen to lay their offerings down.

14

There are Aunty Essie's hands, slender and tapered, twined with veins at the back. There are Martha's dark hands with their milky insides, the marshmallow pads of Aunty Bessie's hands, Nanny's neat hands all sinew and craft. But since they have lost their outline and their colour it is difficult to guess whose are whose. With a vague anonymous music they move through the vapours.

In the diffused light of the doorway Granny Lily's doek can be made out, knotted at the temples; two pink flushes leave her cheeks. She is weighted with a wicker basket full of apricots delivered to her at the door by plump Uncle Eric.

Plump Uncle Eric is spending a good part of the morning up in the apricot tree just under plump Uncle Norman, stripping off the apricots while the branches creak and tremble around them. The squelch of apricots in their mouths is punctuated every now and then by the ping of a pip spat against the corrugated-iron fence or, even more impressive, over the fence and onto the cement slab of the next-door yard.

Granny Lily steps into the thick of the steam. She has plotted all this down to the last ladle of syrup, the last little Tate and Lyle man with his broad-faced shield and his sword proclaiming that out of the strong came forth sweetness. She has planned it all so that by the time the steam has drifted out and the pots are upside down on the old stone sink, by the time everyone has taken off her hair-net and wants tea, the last apricot is sitting perfectly suspended in its jar in a glaze of juice and contemplation.

Granny Lily is gone, Grandpa Joe is gone, Great-aunt Bessie is going. Great-uncle Charlie is gone, so are his wife Vivian and her peppery voice, his sister Eva and her husband and her husband's name. Great-uncle Louis has smoked his last cigar, although the wings of his impeccable moustache still hover over the silver cups on the mantelpiece. Grandpa Joe's brothers and sisters are gone or ignored or forgotten; no one mentions Great-grandmother Dvorah any more.

That leaves Great-aunt Essie, who has lived in their spare rooms and stood at their gravesides, gathered her things up and moved on. With each death her proud face has lost more of its shy hope, cloud has traced more firmly the rims of her irises, her voice has reached more deeply into the soil, a husky astringent male voice run through with milk.

That leaves Aunty Essie to stay with Aunty Bessie, in Aunty Bessie's flat, with Aunty Bessie's amnesia and the faulty hearing-aid which Aunty Bessie forgets to put on, Aunty Bessie's unsteady legs to add to her own; at each of their steps the ground thins to a tightrope and they must balance all their bones one on top of the other to get across.

But Aunty Essie has lost none of her wakefulness; from the winter light in her misty eyes all the way down to the big bevelled sapphire ring on her finger she is still waiting for something better.

One afternoon I ask her about Russia. 'Russia? What can I tell you about Russia? I was so small, you know, just a little girl.' We clear away the jumper stuck with knitting needles, a dog-eared epic, Bessie's pill-box and the pot of grape jam, and Essie brings out the photographs.

16

There she is dodging the pedestrians in the middle of town. Her fur cape, clasped at the neck, squares her shoulders; she has leather gloves in one hand and squeezes a bag under her arm. Her elegance is countered by the pinch of her mouth and eyes, which strain far ahead, taking her chin with them. She hasn't got a minute to lose. There she is, a girl with ankles coyly crossed and upper teeth released in a smile, in the shirt and shorts of a scout, complete with safari hat and riding switch. There she is on the frontier of womanhood, in a string of pearls, her features as smooth as a reflection in still water.

There is Granny Lily on the beach, keeping her dark hair down and frowning. She looks ponderous, and lost. She holds a straw hat before her, a shield crowned with flowers. Beside her Grandpa Joe is dapper and suave, with a victorious smile and one white shoe in the ambit of her flounced dress. Houses climb the mountains of Muizenberg behind them; nannies steer their charges from the sea.

Great-grandmother Dvorah and her husband are on a wooden verandah hemmed by a balustrade; iron poles lift the roof high above them, letting in quantities of breath and light. Seated, her skirt fastened high and falling stiffly to the floorboards, she looks a wily battle-axe who would swing out at the photographer if he made a false move. Her husband is on his feet backing her, but even given his three-piece suit and chaffing glance he does not supercede her stature. He could waggle his goatee and she would not be amused.

The foliage of Granny Lily's garden surrounds everyone; in the glare their eyes fill with shadow. Great-grandmother Dvorah is older still, an unsexed bulk wrapped in black. She would go well with a carving knife, grinning like that. Next to her is the waxclear loveliness of my mother-to-be. Granny Lily's hand rests lightly on Dvorah's arm, the dimple already set in her forehead, the dash of her smile between brackets. Aunty Essie is on the other side, waiting, in black, with little jewelled peacock fans glittering above each breast.

But there is not a single one of Russia. 'Russia?' The maid brings in the tea tray, Aunty Essie spoons grape jam into her cup and the dark fruit wafts down through amber, trailing its syrup. 'You know, it was such a long time ago. The only thing I remember is going up onto the boat, and standing on the deck; as we moved off, I pulled out a clean white handkerchief, and waved goodbye.'

Grandpa Zalman is on guard duty. He climbs out of his icy trench and goes to stand at the tree indicated to him by his officer. Once under this tree he steps on a dead man buried in the snow. He moves on to a second tree, but here also he discovers a dead man, and at a third tree the same.

So he returns to the first tree and stands guard, in the boots that are grafting themselves to his feet, in his greatcoat, in the mud, among searchlights and poisoned wells and the whining of bullets. In the field before him other soldiers frisk the bloated, disfigured dead, joking and squabbling over their pickings. He would rather shoot at them than at any enemy.

But he doesn't budge. The months pass, the bodies pile up and melt into the mud, the villages go by upside down and emptied of everything but a few half-rotten potatoes. Walls topple around him, a cow explodes. The Carpathians rise and fall under bullets, countries change their names and their shapes and he is still there, hoping that one of the other sides will save him by taking him prisoner.

He sits down to have tea with his comrades. There is no water so they fill a pot with snow, and set it on a woodfire in a trench. They search their pockets: no sugar. Tea-leaves are unheard of. Well, hot water is better than nothing.

He stands up and a bullet flies so close that he smells its urgency, feels its shadow burning on his cheek. He has to lie down. Around his neck he has two pouches. In one there is his medical kit: a wad of cotton wool, a bandage, and a safety-pin. In the other there is the name of his next of kin.

A wagon draws up and it is Easter. Out comes an empty aluminium egg for everyone, a handkerchief resembling one of the allies' flags, a small bar of soap and a few sweets, all stamped with the name of the Tzar's mother, Maria Feodorovna. There is also a picture of the Tzar himself, handing a soldier an aluminium egg, and a picture of the Tzarina dressed up as a nurse, bending over a soldier in a hospital bed.

A second wagon draws up, piled with letters and parcels. Everyone assembles hopefully, but when a name is called out the immediate response is: 'Ah, he's already dead, he's already dead.' The parcels are distributed to those soldiers who happen to be closest. They are half-empty anyway.

An officer calls for volunteers to patrol enemy territory and Grandpa Zalman puts his name down, hoping to be caught. But the officer's superior officer won't accept Jews on such a crucial patrol. So he continues to stand, and the mud rises up to his knees, dragging at his coat till he cuts off the hem.

The rabbi's words pass through his mind: 'Be soldiers according to your conscience.' The rabbi is wearing a long black robe hung with medals which clink together as he speaks. The Jewish soldiers on their way to the front start laughing, and the Russian battalion officer laughs a little too.

He starts running. Everyone is running. Behind him there are fields of bedraggled soldiers, all retreating in different directions. A boot factory folds up in yellow smoke. They are ordered to load their rifles, but they are packed too closely together in a narrow street, bumping into each other, shouting, swearing under enemy fire.

20

He runs, despite the sharp pains in his feet, until he sees those who have already passed him come running back. They are surrounded. He crawls through a fence into a yard, where soldiers are lying on the ground with their rifles by their side, waiting. He lies down with them. Four men arrive on horseback, Hussars, wearing red trousers and peaked red hats, blue jackets and gleaming boots. He is made a prisoner of war at last.

★

Grandpa Zalman has a dream. He hobbles along in its company, among hundreds of other prisoners. A woman screams from a window that their captors should whip them as hard as the townspeople were whipped by the Russians. A Jew softly wishes them luck from the side of the road, hoping his children have met with no worse fate at the hands of the Russians.

They march on, grimy, dispirited, empty-handed, light-headed with hunger. Days go by, filled with complaints, ruined fields, crows. Then, in a shimmering cloud of colours, a wagon appears on the horizon. They follow it with a single glance. There is a pyramid of lemons, and oranges, and slabs of chocolate. They rush the wagon only to be knocked back by the rifle-butts of their captors.

Prison camps open their gates to them. The days go grey. They work in grey fields, saw the wood of grey trees: if they won't they are strung up, wrists roped behind them, and faint with the pain.

In the morning, they each receive half a small, bitter corn

loaf. Some gulp it down there and then, leaving nothing for the rest of the day. Some wait till the afternoon, some till the evening, when they chew it a mouthful at a time. Some nibble all day long. They speak of little besides food.

The dream grows. It puts on a bracelet of plaited hair and bright stones picked out of the dust. It lines its eyes with what the others have seen and done. It dabs on the perfume of fresh-sawn planks and makes for the icy mountains bristling with light, where no bullet pierces the young white winds, and no bayonet points at the path. The dream returns to Grandpa Zalman, slender and tinkling like a pine tree.

He receives a letter from his father: 'The Tzar has been dethroned, the nation has the upper hand.' The prisoners are filled with wonder and confusion. There are those who don't dare believe the news, and those who don't want to. Months pass before they are sent back to Russia, in a train of fifty carriages with engines at both ends, to see for themselves.

★

Grandpa Zalman comes into Minsk with his dream. He embraces his mother and his sister, but his father's place is empty and his father is dead.

Gangs comb the streets, shear off the sidelocks of old Jews and drag down their trousers. Queues twist out of those shops which are still intact. All night the houses are sealed, people sleep with iron bars by their side. Bullets mark out the city limits. In the morning the houses are smouldering heaps of rubble. The water-carts stand useless, their horses cut loose.

The Germans have left Minsk, the Bolsheviks are held responsible for the misery. But the Poles are advancing, and the people eagerly await the Poles. The Poles enter the city wearing elegant uniforms, their leaders on horseback. They are applauded. They loot the shops and molest the pedestrians. The situation is soon worse than before.

But the Bolsheviks are advancing, and the people eagerly await the Bolsheviks. They enter the city without shoes or coats, bony and desperate. They are soon in Polish uniforms, and the Poles are walked through the street while the people look on murderously.

Grandpa Zalman is called up to the army by the Bolsheviks. He arranges for another man to attend the medical examination in his name. Since this man has no teeth, a hernia, a feeble heart and pasty skin, he is duly exempted, and Grandpa Zalman receives in the post a list of all his terrible ailments. Not knowing what else to do, he dresses up in a blue suit and tries his hand at selling saccharine on the black market.

★

Grandpa Zalman is walking through his dream. It is quite early in the morning. His brother and sister whisper goodbye as they all approach the Minsk border post. He leaves it behind feeling the beady eyes of rifles on his back.

After a while he stops, not knowing which way to go. Towns sharp with soldiers move behind the forests and the hills.

Mouths open and darkness comes out of them, filling the

23

dream. Where does he come from, he is asked, and why has he forged his papers? A lamp is switched on. A silver pistol flashes at his mouth. Everything he owns is taken from him. He walks on.

He passes a city of migrants. Everyone in the street is carrying a package wrapped in string, even the babies hold little packages in their pudgy hands. Only the bureaucrats in this city ever sit down, the others all fall asleep in queues waiting for their papers. When it is his turn, he says he comes from the city he is trying to reach.

Trees grow in his dream and he has to saw them down. The dream turns a corner and he catches a train, it turns blue and he catches a boat. It grows rock-solid. He locates a crack and plants dynamite in it, then walks around in the blazing sun with his companions, picking up the pieces.

With a special hammer they chip at these pieces, knocking them into the ground to make a long road. Arabs on camels help them cart the pieces further along. They sit there getting blisters on their fingers, gashes, burns. Some give up.

But Grandpa Zalman tucks his head in and concentrates on this new task. At the end of the road stands Granny Toba. She is so beautiful that just for a while Grandpa Zalman stops walking.

Granny Toba stands wailing at her kitchen door in Petach Tiqva. Morning light is in her high-combed hair and satin dressing-gown; the proud worn lions of her beauty toss and storm around.

The family crowds into the kitchen, where jars of luminous red quinces line the shelves and the air is rinsed with the smell of cucumbers Granny Toba has been dicing for breakfast. At length she quietens down and announces that another turkey has just died.

The last in a long procession of animals and catastrophes winding its way behind Granny Toba from Minsk to Palestine, from there to Johannesburg and back, this particular turkey joins a whole ghostly troop of Petach Tiqva turkeys and chickens which have insisted on dying, even when they weren't at the end of their lives.

Next come the jackals, through the scrub just across the sand road, cutting the night to ribbons with the blades of their crying. Granny Toba is roused from sleep by the vigorous gobbling of her turkeys. Immediately she envisions a turkey pogrom, jackals with gory snouts stepping between the lifeless fowls.

'Oh my God, Zalman,' she moans, 'go and see.' He finds the turkeys pecking away at their corn as merrily as beggars at a wedding feast, kept awake by the electric light that Granny Toba had forgotten to switch off.

Before the jackals, the Johannesburg chickens: she roves around the chicken-run with a bottle of castor oil in her hand, keeping a sharp look-out for any chicken which seems out of sorts. Every now and then she grabs one, wedges its maddened body firmly against her, and forces some castor oil down its raw orange gullet. Granny Toba has the liveliest chicken-run in the neighbourhood.

Then she hears that a poultry disease is doing the rounds, and promptly scrubs all her chickens down with a solution of ammonia. After this she notices that their heads are drooping, so she gives them some castor oil for good measure. They die anyway.

'Johannesburg,' says Granny Toba wryly, her hair massing into a cloud as her face goes glum, 'what were we doing in Johannesburg? For twenty years we sat on our suitcases, waiting to get back to Palestine.'

She lights the Friday-night candles and all around eyes open in the sepia air, wistful and smouldering in their heavy lids, while the walls hold back wastes of snow deaf and endless as the dead.

★

On Saturday morning Granny Toba's brother Peretz falls ill from a surfeit of berberries. Berberries grow at the side of the fields, and the toiling peasants pop a few into the mouths of their children to keep them mildly drunk and out of trouble. But Peretz has taken an overdose, and is soon in a coma.

'We must find a purgative,' urges Granny Toba's mother. But her father won't hear of saddling a horse on the Sabbath. 'And anyway,' he adds, 'the child is only sleeping.'

The mother goes off to fetch the Rabbi, who tells her stubborn husband that life is more sacred than the Sabbath. At which he simply shakes his beard. So she borrows a Christian horse and cart and rides off to Minsk, Toba by her side and Peretz lying limply between them.

Halfway there he comes to, looks around blearily and asks where they are going. They continue to Minsk anyway; there Granny Toba's mother buys something cheap and harmless from a chemist to salve her conscience. Some weeks later, in the middle of a meal and despite all previous cautioning, Peretz brightly recounts the whole episode.

Granny Toba's father is a schochet. She hides under the table and watches while he blows up a cow's lung, looking it over for blue or red blemishes, or any other sign that the cow's meat is not good. On the table are all his sacred knives. At the far side of the room, the cow's owner anxiously paces up and down.

Cows come into the big wooden house, and go out leaving their hides behind to be rubbed with salt and rolled up in barrels. Later, the hides are bartered for bread and cheese.

There is a wood-fire under the bath in the big wooden house, and a bed over the oven. There are barrels of berries and cucumbers pickling in the cellar. There are shreds of precious orange peel in the vinegar. There are slabs of ice cut from the river to keep everything fresh.

In comes a boy in his Friday-night best. Granny Toba, who has been told to put on her prettiest white-lace dress, and is given no answer when she asks why, sits as far away from

27

him as possible. His sidelocks shine in the candle-light as he looks at her, meaningfully. Then he turns to her father, who looks at her, meaningfully. She ducks under the table and crawls out.

Her uncle the cartage contractor stops his horse and cart at the door and in comes a cupboard peppered with holes. The children crowd around, wondering why another cupboard is needed in the house. Inside they see the flickering eyes of a Tzarist official who is being delivered from the Bolsheviks.

Epidemics are spreading everywhere. In come Bolsheviks, making sure all the sick have been taken off to isolation wards. Out goes Granny Toba's mother with a compress on her forehead to distract them from Granny Toba, who is down in the cellar with scarlet fever.

In come more Bolsheviks. On discovering Granny Toba they say it's not girls they want, only gold. 'My daughters are gold to me,' says Granny Toba's mother softly. They leave with the sacred knives and scrolls.

In they come again and out goes the whole family, out to where trenches fill up with the naked dead while wrinkles multiply on the wary faces of the spared. Wolves fatten behind birch trees, churches leap up to heaven in long red flames.

But the young lions of Granny Toba's beauty lead her elsewhere, they grow at the head of the procession of her life, licking her tears and flexing their muscles as they carry her across the acid soil of the tundra to the edge of the sea.

And they enter the arching grey waters. Ships pass them by, returning from Palestine full of painful voices. 'There is no hope where we have been,' say the voices, 'it is all drudgery and sand.'

But the pull of the far shore is greater than any complaint. And so at length Granny Toba is delivered to a land of chickens and turkeys, eggs and death, where the leaves of the trees are as new as the eyes of survivors, and the tree-trunks as old as those who have lived other lives.

The trees knit their soft blue needles together on the hills; they gird themselves with swagging aromatic branches and taper up over bleached waves of sand. They swell secretly with oranges in the glossy darkness, dance a cracked and bumpy old dance, going off balance and pausing for centuries.

Skinny and restless they line the roads, reeking of ointment for sore muscles; light sparks off their sickle leaves. They lean quietly together before the houses while birds with jet bodies hop through them.

Their roots draw up from pale clay and thin black threads of water, from the dreams of dead forests, from middens of bones and beards and suitcases, wounds, pickled cucumbers, kisses and keys and words that have mouldered into earth; from the minerals and gasses and salts of exile the roots draw their sustenance and wind into the firmness of the trunk.

The trees bear their knots and their rings, the sap in their callused skins, preparing the furled multitude of their memories for the sky.

On the hills at the approach to Jerusalem they knit their soft blue needles together. Blown-out motor cars mount boulders among them, look blankly about, and prepare for flight. The trees reach through their charred window frames, and stitch the spirit of the lost riders back into the ground.

II Window

The sea: does not wash the side of Johannesburg our city, no wave unrolls there for purposes of commerce, delight, or the discarding of sins at the propitious time.

We set out to reach the sea in a little grey Morris Minor with a picture of an ox and three blue ripples on the hooter, and a number of horses in the engine which will not pull. It takes fourteen hours there and a few more back, not counting breakdowns.

In my bag are three bottles to be filled with sea-water for Clubfoot Izzy who works the petrol pumps across the road. He says it's for Enema, no doubt the name of his wife. I hand the bottles to him feeling like an emissary from another world.

To Johannesburg, only storms bring waters of any noise and consequence. They take hours to gather themselves up hot and sombre; from one end of the clouds to the other they thunder around bearing jagged branches of lightning, and for long seconds turn the air pale with revelation.

Then the rain gobs down, hail goes for greengages and apricots hanging from their twigs, hammers on roofs, shoots window panes. Grass jumps with hail, ice ghoens and glassies shatter and melt into each other piling white and deep enough to make an iceman.

The city is purled with water. A river surges down our road, licking red earth from pavement flower-beds, making much bubble and fuss at plane boles, split-pole fences, car bumpers, turning its back on the flat-footed houses and the pocked swimming-pools as it heads for the metal screams of the peacocks in the zoo.

But it does not last. Inch by inch it lowers itself down the storm-water drains until only a rumour of roaring continues underground. Meanwhile steam twists and stiffens on the tar, releasing the pungency of split rock.

Out come snails, horns first down their silver slides, out come water-logged worms, and birds. Out come boys and girls in galoshes to mash all the puddles; muttering gardeners, the mute sun.

Blunt towers come down from the skies; below them the Ridge of White Waters dries up. The city forgets the flood and remembers its gold; at the side of the road the dust grows bold.

Flying ants: rise from nests in wet earth, brushing frenzied, glassy wing-blades. They enter the washed evening air in a haywire pillar of whispers, cutting light from the cones of the streetlamps, laying out wings in a glitter behind them. The wingless scurry off on tender egg-bellies across tar and grass.

All windows and doors must be latched, and meshed frames fastened against them, before they come percussing the house. Nervous spiders and moths, even dive-bombing rose-beetles, give way to them. They laminate porch and sill with wings, and still there are enough to come flying at the panes. Only a switched-off light makes for pause in their enquiry.

By one means or another, some gain entry. Against walls and hot globes they delicately thresh and collapse, cross the floor brown and unbeautiful and smooth to the thumb, spewing pasty goo when popped underfoot.

Not all survivors are found and ushered out. They slip under straw mats, behind paintings, through old knots in the floor-boards. Somewhere not far away must be the promised earth in which to raise a family.

They thread the house with their searching as we fall asleep. Down in the cellar their forebears the termites, already well installed, gnaw upwards into our dreams.

The stapelia plant: has fat glaucous fingers for leaves, tinged with purple at the nodules. It bunches up in shadow at the bottom of the rockery, away from its weird neighbours: cotyledons with leaves the colour of silver milk, waxed over and lined with a blood-vessel; matted white shag of Old Man's Beard; lithops that emerge mottled foot-pads first, and hold little flowers between their toes.

From the wall behind the rockery, Golden Dew opens long throats to the bees; above it, bruised and swollen figs bring red-eyed mousebirds screeching until their beaks are jammed with fig meat. But down below, the stapelia plant keeps discreetly to itself.

On Sundays I am out doing the rockery with my father, hauling up more rocks and spading humus mixed with earth between them. And while my father fills holes with hums and grunts and stringy succulent roots, I glean weeds, or sit on rocks to ease them in a bit further.

When the rockery is finished for the day we stand before it and douse it with water. The earth darkens and smells roasted, sighing like an animal in sleep. Rocks jut through, glazed and new.

One morning a magnificent stink swarms up from the rockery; it could be carrion or cat rut or warm frothing yeast. But it comes from the stapelia plant, which has unfurled a five-tipped star of leathery old petal against the ground, all jaded greys and maroon and gold. Wrinkled and hairy, it has at its centre an unspeakable hole with all manner of insects crawling in and out.

This continues for days. Even when the show folds up the odour lingers around the stapelia plant, which grows on unremarkably in the shadow of its rock at a rate of maybe four nodules a year.

The books: are more numerous than the bricks in the walls. They go up to the moulded-steel ceiling and down to the floor in each room of the house, pressed together pensively and turning their backs on us all. From this position they exert their powers.

Feet begin to drag in their presence, hands reach out for them with slow compulsion. Faces which finally dip into them emerge with a far-off look. Readers drift backwards book in hand, feeling with calves for the edge of a chair; upon contact they sink in a coma through the cushions.

The books slip into bed, into the bathroom and the car. Some disappear, whereupon swart glances fall on suspects; curses follow in their wake. It is always the missing books which are particularly needed. Certain conversations cannot be completed in their absence, and speakers are left open-mouthed in mid-sentence before a gap in the shelf where one was last seen.

On Saturday afternoons books are placed on the table in the middle of the coiled yellow grass carpet. The door opens to admit people of all shapes, sizes and colours who are soon seated around the table. The books pass between them, voices are lowered, and bulging smoke-columns rise up from the chairs. Meanwhile the door must be sealed because of the bug that lives in the telephone at the far end of the passage.

Some books must be meticulously fitted into suitcases and tea-crates, sprinkled with rat poison, moth-balls and D.D.T., and stowed away in the most obscure regions of the house. On Sundays a few of these are brought out and taken to the spot behind Lizzy's room where my father and I are to perform the last rites.

The books are laid out on the ground, opened in the middle, and set alight at all four corners. With sticks we turn the burning pages. The paper crisps and curves upwards, words shine in the spreading blot of darkness as flame licks them to cinder and lifts a few into the sky.

Not a single word must remain. When there are only red filaments crinkling at the edges of the pages, we batter the books softly into a heap of ash.

The ash is then mixed with earth and humus and carried off in a wheelbarrow to be fed to the plants and trees. Each Sunday we carry the ash to a different part of the garden, till it has nourished everything that grows there.

Lizzy's doek: is lopsided, pirate style, right from the start of the day when she leaves her room across the garden. The knot-ends bob at the nape of her neck as she goes down on all fours, dips a rag into the oily whorl of the Cobra tin, and rubs tomato-red rings into the cold porch floor.

It is still there as she gets the silver to gleam and airs her bunions out on the grass, irons damp sheets till the steam rolls out, takes a break over a mug of weak tea and a few slabs of jam-smeared Atlas bread.

Burnished with age, Lizzy's doek sits blinking above her interminable tuneless songs; follows her to the edge of the pavement where it sits in line with many smartly starched companions, waiting for the fah-fee man to pull up and hand someone a small fortune.

Lizzy's doek goes with an equally off-colour apron, and slippers which have long collapsed under the horn of her heel. It stays on day in and day out, slips now and then but keeps Lizzy covered all the way back to her room in the evening.

Most of Lizzy's room is occupied by a broad iron bed raised on piles of bricks. On a crate table is a white cloth embroidered with copper and orange flowers, a Gideon's Bible on a doily, a short mirror with some of its mercury peeled away.

An arm of piping stretches from the coal stove up through the corrugated-iron roof and brings in grains of rust and soot. There are patches of damp in the walls, inhabited by bed bugs which can tell when it is early morning and time to bite.

No spray attains the heart of their colony.

One evening I come in there when Lizzy has pulled off her doek. Last light shows an apron on a hook, the green-backed star of her church pinned to the breast of her shapeless dress. I look at her hair, cropped dark and vegetal and close to the skull, finding there no sign of her womanhood, nor anything to replace it. Estrangement comes over me. I can neither speak nor take my eyes away.

I breathe in the reek of paraffin, sweat, a brown-paper cigarette, the fatty sweetness of mielie-pap and mutton steaming in a plate. She regards me quietly from out of her divested face with its deep lineaments, wide cheekbones where the skin stands clear, flat-fleshed lips, missing teeth. I shiver. We say nothing. Whatever it is I came in for, I forget. She watches me leave without moving from her place. We don't wish each other goodnight.

The road at night: is lined with dogs, reclining at their gates as the huge motor cars cruise past. The tar is delicately washed with jasmine, wisteria, marigold, shot through with the sorrow of lions and peacocks down in the zoo. Tripped alarms and sirens twist into their crying. Walls and fences against the road are high, hedges dense. Many trees hold up the moonlight.

Black men slowstep along the road at night, hands empty, hats on, or lunge in a stupor from which broken words burst. One welds with the shadow of a hedge, his steel guitar shivering dark liquid where a few low chords leap over and over. Another is running blind, streetlamps catching the blood on his cheek.

They all cause the dogs to rant and batter at their gates, and whites to stay clear. Weary and racked, or carrying themselves erect with the easy air of owners, they proceed through the night. They are on their way somewhere else, or nowhere at all. They could pick anyone's backyard.

The tar on the road at night keeps the heat of the day. If fresh, it bubbles. Under the streetlamp-jig of mad insects it is bleached the colour of salt. Clawed shadow shifts distractedly against the light.

★

With milkbottles and dog-chains, gate-latches and anxious heels, the road comes rattling and clicking its way into the morning. Birds fill the trees with sweet emergency. A newspaper flies over the hedge and makes a perfect landing, neatly folded, on the lawn.

42

The road reveals its collection of dead little mammals, yields its dew to the sun and Firestone tyres. In the gutter: a molasses glow on the shield of the rhinoceros beetle, battling over feldspar chips, mown grass, pom-pom seedballs. In the stone wall: the hoopoe bird, needle-beak first. In the brick wall: bees.

At the gate the dustman rests for a second, taking stabs of breath, his taut manhood hung with rags. In a single sweep the lid is clanged off the bin, the bin swung to his padded shoulder and he is gone, haunches pumping one one one one one foot past its brother, eyewhites whitened in his mask of ash.

Teeth mashing air, arm locked to his load, he mounts the road, another dustman following and across the block a third going for the drone of the rubbish truck, which is always further and further on. The gate is full of him again, the lid tolls once on the empty bin, falls off with a din.

On the road in the morning: thin trails of paw-paw skin, steak bones, warm coals, eggshell, freshly torn bits of hedge.

★

The school crest: is divided into four coloured quadrants. Red backs a crown with three gold branches, yellow an open book; blue, a scroll of parchment about to eat a plume; green, two tapes running under an archbishop's mitre: Alfred, Bede, Caedmon and Dunstan, who came from England a long time ago.

There is one crest sewn to my navy-blue cap, another to my

navy-blue blazer. Blazer and pants pockets, if not burst, are fat with marbles, the odd coppery pupa that wiggles at the tip, jumping bean, lump of pink sweet.

My eye is out for beetles and other passers-by; watching, always watching, with silence for a tower. The skin down my legs is tattooed by mosquitoes, scratched to blood before I know it.

On the road in the morning: the mulberry tree where I dream of letting all my silkworms loose; ivory seeds in spongy canna pods, good for pea-shooters; a few nannies walking Grade Ones and Twos, in icing-coloured aprons and crimped white caps that bring out the chocolate of their skins. They have names like Regina, Patience, Angelina, Evelina.

Morning glories thread through the fences, tender violet-tongued trumpets that fit over the nose. Breathe in and the petal flesh plugs the nostrils, bringing fragrance up behind the face, cutting out air.

In garden after garden swimming-pools blow wobbly bubbles up through cool blue depths. Men with smooth jowls snooze down driveways in low-slung highly waxed motor cars. Their elbows jut out of the windows, voices address them over the radio. The men are soon lined up along the road, with their windows closed and the voices raised.

One driver doesn't edge forward fast enough for the driver behind him, who reaches down into his glove compartment and pulls out a gun. A grey angel watches from an archway, bees swarming under wing.

Brenda's house: has at least two immaculate storeys, with no tree or creeper to encumber the salmon-pink walls. The tall split-pole fence around it stinks of pitch, the palings let no light through. A sign screwed to the gate-post bears the legend 'Pluto Alarm Systems' below the head of a dog with black spots and a flat eye.

From the garden comes a sound of water falling in gouts. Sometimes, leaves rustle. Just once a grey limousine slides out, without Brenda. Behind it I glimpse fluted cream columns, tar chips and a few rose bushes whose branches make cracks against the sheen of the walls. Then the gates close, and someone crunches slowly away.

Brenda arrives at school by unknown means, freckled and quiet and smiling with her eyes. She plays netball, for Bede. We don't notice each other at all.

★

Marbles: alies malies ghoens glassies puries smokies ironies twos castles tens twenties shy up its not counted if you don't toe the line toe the line! Right. Everything under the sun and nix for you. Pockets biscuit-tins cigar-boxes bank-bags grimy hands full of marbles and the glass chatter of marbles you're too crack give me my marbles back I never said you could shy give them back! Drops? Tish? OK, ghoen-ghoen tish.

Four paces for a castle fifteen for a twenty little bits of grit strewn strategically in front of the glittering prize. Paul Salko sits in a line of others before the library bushes fat legs forked open a ten of bright ironies between them, everyone raining marbles at him all at once from miles away, backs almost against the hall wall. Meanwhile Paul Salko's gang is in the bushes, hunting down whatever his bulk of body fails to stop.

A marble snicks the pyramid but glances off leaving it intact and the gang advances, pushing everyone away. A second marble topples half the pyramid but no one can decide whose marble it was. Wild fists and scuffles are interrupted by the bell.

We run across the marble patch pounding powdery bottoms, stamping sandals as our cooped up marbles collide. Clouds of dust accompany us to class. And there in line are Leonie Hofmeyr and Karen Waldman, Naomi Beneishowitz and Merle Korp. There is Brenda. They are standing calmly, polished all the way down to their white socks. Not even ink spots seem to get them.

★

The wagons: are on the move as first light breaks and the mountains climb down from the sky. Their wheels leave dark slots in the mercury grass, steaming dung and hullabaloo come from the cattle and sheep pressing about them.

The people in the wagons test their whips between the horns of the oxen, adjust their bonnets, and wash their eyes in the new air. It is going to be another brilliant day on their way north. Someone begins to sing:

Janpierewiet, Janpierewiet, Janpierewiet staan stil,
Janpierewiet, Janpierewiet, Janpierewiet draai om.
Goeie môre my vrou, hiers 'n soentjie vir jou,
Goeie môre my man, daar is koffie in die kan.

Behind the wagons is the wild green sea, and at the sea stands Jan van Riebeeck, his luxuriant hair flowing out in the breeze. There is goffered lace down his breast, his calves are moulded by gleaming boots, his palm rests lightly on the pommel of his sword. Around him are all the carrots and tomatoes and cucumbers that he came to plant in 1652.

There are also stinkwood trees, yellow-wood trees, spittoons and slave-bells, white gables and white grapes and brown people whose bellies stick forward and whose bottoms stick backwards and who have arrived from just the other side of the mountains to meet Jan van Riebeeck, the first man at the Cape.

Then the British land, and hand out Bibles, and get everyone to speak English and be free. So the people in the wagons, who were Dutch but are now Voortrekkers, load up with concertinas and coffee and rusks and muskets and Bibles of their own, yoke their oxen, and head north.

They stop at nothing. They slit up lions for shoes and trousers, and festoon their wagons with drying meat. With pangas they hack through thorn and scrub. When a mountain appears the wagon wheels roll off, the canvas roofs flap up like sails and bit by bit everything drifts over the peaks. On the other side the wagons fit together again, and buckle down to the business of getting further away from the British.

There is no one else on the land they cross, though every now and then they come across a kraal with a black king in it who has a lot of wives lying on floors made of dung and ox-blood. Meanwhile, tribes are marauding their way down Africa, trampling on all the thorns and scorpions with their bare feet and advancing in the form of ox-heads.

Horns of warriors curve across the land with assegais and giant shields, as quietly as grass. Against their onslaught the Voortrekkers hitch all wagons into a laager, cramming the gaps with branches of thorn-bush and mimosa. While the women and children ram powder down muskets and sing hymns, the men fire at the black breasts of the enemy.

When it is all over the rivers run red with blood and the Voortrekkers, who are slowly becoming Boers, pick assegais out of their wagons. They make pledges and vows and covenants. The leaders give their names to mountains and cities and public swimming-pools.

Each year the wagons rattle and strain out of the Cape, led by intrepid men whose wives wear coal-scuttle bonnets to keep their cheeks pink and whose children are born with nerves of steel. Each year we follow them until they are white dots in the distance, becoming Afrikaners while the British – now known as the English – wage a small war on them and then everyone becomes European.

The marauding tribes, who are the cause of Kaffir Wars and later become Natives and Bantu, line up for health inspection and go down to work in the mines. Finally there is a Republic, and the whole school gets bronze medals and flags and sings about blue heaven with kranses in it.

Our class goes down to the museum in the middle of town, to find out a bit more about the story. There is an ox-wagon whose thick wooden frame is charred and pocked under its beeswax. There are Chinese dice, and pictures of Chinese miners wearing headbands and looking sullen. There is a stuffed Bushman with a shrunken leathery skin standing in some sand in a glass case.

Just before lunch-time Eleanor Lambeth has an epileptic fit. She lies on the floor next to the ox-wagon, ice-white and triangular with her eyeballs working under their lids, knee-caps protruding. Every now and then her body shudders. Her tongue has slipped down her throat, and our teacher and the librarian hunt everywhere for a soup-spoon so they can fish it out.

★

The Duplessis's: are all orange. They slip out of bed in uncreased orange pyjamas, and arrive simultaneously at the breakfast table neatly dressed for the day. They smile at each other, and tuck into a steaming orange breakfast. After-wards, Meneer Duplessis drives off in his car, and Hennie and Sarie wheel their bicycles to the gate, while Mevrou Duplessis in an orange polka-dot apron waves Totsiens to them all from the front door.

Meneer Duplessis walks into his orange office, where he has an iron filing-cabinet, an orange secretary, a clock and a window with an orange cloud in it. Meanwhile, Hennie and Sarie are in class. They have taken off their blazers, and lean cool as cucumbers over their exercise books. Then the bell rings, and they dive into the orange school pool.

By evening the Duplessis's are together again, waiting for supper as orange as ever. They are there every time our teacher, Mrs M, unrolls them, clearing her throat and tapping at them with her cane so that they dimple and sway a bit. This is the signal for us to strike up a frame by frame commentary, in Afrikaans, which we do with a lot of vigorous rhythm and a few shaky phrases that trail in the wake of Mrs M's booming cues.

Mrs M is puffy and stout. Her hair is red, and her pets in the front desks have to go up and tease it every now and then. Heaving under a sunset sky-line frieze of oxwagons, kranses, umbrella trees and women with clay pots on their heads, she conducts us through the Duplessis day.

Several lessons later, after we have thankfully seen Hennie and Sarie off to bed, Mrs M sends the class monitor off to fetch a fresh roll of Duplessis. She pulls on the ring at the end of the string and there they are again, only this time they are all blue, and it is Saturday morning.

We get no more than a glimpse of Hennie, who is helping an old blue lady across the street, when Mrs M realises with a start that Afrikaans should be over, it is time for Hygiene. Tomorrow we will have to go faster, to catch up with the syllabus.

★

Ronald: has trouble easing into his desk and trouble easing out of it, trouble with his buttons and trouble with the stairs. He gets both feet onto one step before attempting the next; flesh trembles along his tapering legs till he stops to dab the

50

sweat from his brow.

He takes no part in marbles, bullfights, knifey-knifey, red rover or king stingers. All break he is out on the grey slate patio, chewing on sandwiches and jam doughnuts and surveying the chaos.

Only once does he bring his costume and towel with him when the class goes down to the swimming-pool. Hot-faced he emerges from the change-rooms into the unsparing sunlight, his breasts gazing down at the pinkness that swells up under a feint blue net of veins. The next time he brings a note, gets scowled at, and is allowed to go and sit on the stands.

We are in the hall one afternoon after school helping to set chairs out for a meeting when, through the pandemonium, a deliberate series of bangs is heard coming from the direction of the stage. The stage curtains jerk apart and an apparition drifts into view, swaddled in heavy plum-coloured curtain cloth and topped by a school cap, inside out so that only the shiny black lining shows.

In the middle of the stage it comes to a stationary position, turns, and waits for silence. 'In my native village in Johannesburg,' it announces at length, 'there is a song that we always sing when a young girl gets married. It's called "The Click Song" by the English, because they cannot say "Qongqothwane".'

It sweeps its way forward, curtain rings in tow, face burning with purpose. Under the row of shields, red for Alfred, yellow for Bede, blue for Caedmon and green for Dunstan, it pauses, hauls in a breath, and begins:

'Igqipa lendlela nguQongqothwane . . .'*

Sweat twinkles from under the black cap, arms hitch the slipped curtain up a few times and otherwise sway this way and that, holding the song out towards us. Everyone is motionless and remains so. Then the apparition sweeps off, and neither foot-stamping nor cheers will bring it back. Those who go to investigate find Ronald already unwrapped and on his hurried way home.

Next day he is out on the grey slate patio again, munching sandwiches and jam doughnuts, surveying the chaos that reigns all break.

* The healer of the road, he is the dung-beetle

Miss Ilse von Pfluck-Hartung: lives in a little old house squashed between honey-brick flats, with a thick, lush jungle for a front garden and an Alsatian called Kaiser in a kennel round the back. She comes to the door with a pack of Pekinese dogs snuffling and woofing and weeing their way past her ankles to investigate any newcomers.

The whole house smells of marrowbones that are simmering on the stove and lying under the piano; the nose is also met by flea-powder, wet carpet, freshly rubbed resin and the box-files of yellowing sheet-music that lie in wait all along the passage.

In the music room someone is usually just finishing a lesson, suspended over the edge of the piano or a violin. In this case I can glibly listen out for mistakes while deciding whether I should break the news to Miss von Pfluck-Hartung that I haven't practised, again, or let her discover this grinding bit of information for herself.

Miss von Pfluck-Hartung is very broad. She has got broad, burly shoulders and broadness where her hips would be if her tubular dresses disclosed them. She has got aluminium-pale hair cut short and square around her broad face, a baby moustache, and a delicate crackling light in her grey eyes.

She sits with her tough fingers on the keys, pressing out a few chords while waiting for me to step over the pekes and set my music on the stand. 'Come on, come on,' she urges, while I stall for time. 'Well, how did it go this week?'

Her words come out precisely tooled by her German diction, but her voice is not unkind. I look down at the mauled, stained, hair-strewn carpet that must once have been brown. I cannot tell a lie, but the truth is somewhat extreme.

I hand her the violin, mentioning a peg which is always slipping and needs to be chalked. Then, when there seems no hope of doing anything else, I begin to bow my way desperately through a forest of smooth-headed, skinny-tailed notes which all squawk at my approach. Miss von Pfluck-Hartung stops me in the middle, and asks if I am not perhaps having problems with my eyesight: I have been screwing up my eyes at the notes as if I had never seen them before.

The lesson continues, and I am in the middle of a rousing if not immediately identifiable rendering of 'Oh for the Wings of a Dove' when the pekes pick themselves up from the carpet and herald in the next victim.

Sometimes, I go with Miss von Pfluck-Hartung down the passage into the spare-room or her bedroom in search of chalk, or resin, or an E-string to replace the one which has fortunately just snapped. There is more of the plastic beechwood wallpaper that lines the music room, framed by deep-stained wooden panels and skirting-boards; more of the smoky, tapering ice-cream globes that must be switched on because honey-brick wall blocks the light from the windows.

There are dog-leashes, hat-boxes, crates topped with rubber drums, rattles, tambourines, triangles, clay cuckoos and castanets for Miss von Pfluck-Hartung's boisterous and unbashful Saturday morning toy orchestra. There are bird-cages, one containing a lonesome blue budgie and a cuttle-bone; a few back numbers of Stern magazine with women lifting big stiff breasts out of the front covers; dog bowls filled

54

with water or mush at the feet of music-stands in various states of collapse.

Stranded in the clutter, backs to the walls, there are bedsteads, commodes and grand wardrobes, carved with flowers and shields and curlicues. They stand foursquare, glimmering darkly out of the dust, forgotten messengers from another world.

★

At the end of the year, when Miss von Pfluck-Hartung's pupils give their concert, the double-doors down one side of the music room are opened out to reveal her immaculate salon. In cram grannies, grandpas, aunts, uncles and other proud and unsuspecting music-lovers, along with disabused mothers and fathers who have all year been caught between the desire to get their children to practise and the consequences for the household when they do.

Afterwards, when everyone is recovering over tea and cake, I go into the salon. There is polished woodwork and plate silver, there are wide shallow bowls planted with cactuses, glazed bridges and pagodas. Opposite the bay windows that look out onto the jungle hang two sepia photographs, stamped with a family crest.

In one there is a castle seen from a distance, shingles, turrets and dormers hoisted above oak trees into the air. In the other there are three children. The little big-boned girl holding her hands over a velvet dress has Miss von Pfluck-Hartung's face; nothing from the ribbons in her hair to the buckles on her shoes has not been starched and pleated into place.

At the end of the afternoon, when it is time to go home, we walk down the steps while Miss von Pfluck-Hartung waves goodbye from the porch, her recently liberated pekes jumping up and down and woofing till they squeak.

I watch the jungle rise up and swallow her, ferns, vines, tendrils taking her body away. Behind a screen of greenery the little girl is left, with one big hand raised, and suffused light settling on her soft helmet of hair.

The Sunday city: is already laid out on the kikuyu grass, away from the shade of the trees, when we get there. Barbers with silver Figaro clippers and slices of mirror apply themselves to bent heads. Photographers pace around rings of gilt-framed portraits, disappear under black cloths and embrace their tripods. In the midst of the city, mountainous blazing green men beat the sky with wicker-work crosses. Heaped against them is their congregation.

There are no walls, no gates, no roads to the city. The nearest sign says 'No Ball Games' and is some way down the kikuyu slope. There are few children, no one who is not black; everyone is dressed up in Sunday best and melted together till the last of the grass-blades goes under.

Men tilt their heads back, take a pinch of snuff, swig at a brown-paper bag. Women with giant thighs cluck and sigh as they thread needles through intricate embroidery. One man strokes a river out of a guitar, another jives into it. Someone holds a head wrapped in a rag. Someone digs cautiously at a corn on a toe.

We wander on down to the Lake, one-eyed peacock feathers shimmering out of Robert's grimy hand, a fat bag of bottle-tops slung over my shoulder. We pass ironed white men on the bowling-green who make their balls curve perfectly.

We pause at the ponds, where tree roots go red and dip into the pitch-thick water, and crabs glimmer like distant head-lamps along the bottom. Everywhere couples walk around on three legs, or stop and squeeze each other till they have no strength left and must lie down. 'Love stories,' says Robert, and rolls his eyes knowingly.

57

At the Lake, families fit themselves into wobbly wooden boats, and retire to the shaded restaurant for milk-shakes and varnished wedges of tart. Ducks waddle out of the weedy goo of the water, barking for crusts.

When the light weakens, the spray of the fountain in the Lake turns mint green, pink and cherry red. There are still a few boats on the water. The cormorants glide in to roost in the trees that throng the island. They flap their wings out before folding them up, and hook their dark throats into the sky.

It is time to go home, dribbling pine cones, keeping an eye open for rare bottle-tops. At the bowling-green we slow down and look about. There is nothing left of the Sunday city, nothing but a large area of squashed grass and a few empty snuff-tins.

Further on we see some of the inhabitants of the city, in aprons or overalls, crimped hats, tackies. It is nearly Monday, and they have begun leading their other lives.

III   Watcher

The blacks cross the field to the wire fence, tens of hundreds of them, line it, lean over it, wince into the sunshine. There are broad ladies under parasols, young men punching the air, an old man punting himself along on a walking-stick. They wait. They have got all day. Someone should be arriving at the police-station any second now to address them, a man from the government.

Saracen tanks roll down the road. A policeman manning one waves from the hatch. Blacks wave back. The tanks roll into the police-station grounds.

The blacks are running. Youths, women, breasts swung to one side, doeks gone skew, one man mounting a bicycle, two boys together, arms intersecting in flight. Some twisted round in interest, some in laughter, some in disbelief, one doing a dance step, they advance across the stubble and the clumps of long grass.

At their backs, behind the fence, policemen stand on tanks, sten guns and revolvers lengthening out of them. One bends to reload.

In the road: bodies, fallen, feet towards the fence, clothes blotting up blood; a litter of shoes, bags, hats, bicycles. Some of the fallen prop themselves up, a priest holds a jar of water to the lips of a man soon dead. In the background: two horses and a foal, heavy old cars with narrow windows.

Further down the road: survivors, looking over their shoulders. White policemen in peaked caps and blacks in topis leave the confines of the fence. They carry sten guns, revolvers, a sjambok. The survivors walk on.

Heaped against the wire fence: hats, soft felt hats, slouch hats, a stetson, a beret, crushed, upside down, filled with sunlight; a Basotho hat, a sun hat, coats, a blanket, a punctured parasol, odd shoes, one with eyelets up to the ankle. A policeman stands there, bare burnt arm down past holster to rifle butt.

Sharpeville, 21 March 1960: 'The tree of freedom is watered with blood.'

Again I sit at the bookshelf, locked in the images: death reaches among the bright-eyed runners, dead and living still together. Next plate, the pick has been made. The holes in the backs of the fallen are clean, blood seeps from their stomachs into the ground.

★

The book is wrapped in the dust-cover of Stendhal's *The Red and the Black*, wedged two rows behind a stout cordon of tomes; it is, not surprisingly, overlooked by the Special Branch men when they come round for a visit.

In fact, they don't have much luck at all. Not a stick of dynamite, not a measly pamphlet in sight. Nothing, until they discover the bell-buttons. There is an excess of bell-buttons in the house, sometimes as many as three to a room: the senior Branch man is convinced he is on to something. He gets into a huddle with his raw-eared cronies, and soon they are tracing wires up and down the house. Maybe the whole city is webbed with an alarm system, maybe big bells have been set up somewhere to chime the revolution into life. The four men are quite beside themselves, crawling along the beading in different directions with their tails up.

One of them arrives at the passage cupboard where his wire
disappears under the door. He asks imperiously for the key,
only to find a small bell with no clapper hanging limply
above provisions of carbolic soap and toilet rolls. Then a yelp
comes from the garden and all four of them are on the tracks
of a wire that runs around the back of the house. Hands
craving for their holsters, they stop short at Lizzy's room. The
wire has been snipped off below the window.

'What's all these wires about?' they demand. But my mother
cannot enlighten them. The previous occupants apparently
needed bells so as never to feel alone, not at table, in bed or
in the bath. More than that she does not know. But taking
advantage of the febrile hunt she has assembled a few hot
documents and hidden them under the mattress of the bed
where my brother is fast asleep.

'If you go in there he'll wake up and scream his lungs out.
There is absolutely no way to quieten him down.' At will, my
mother can pierce the thickest skull with her words.

The Special Branch men continue their fruitless search of the
house, missing out my brother's room and tiptoeing every
time they pass it by.

★

Rarely does my mother find the time to read about anything but microbes or glands or hermaphrodites; each night she raids books full of them, taking rapid notes in her insect scrawl while chewing on apples and nuts for fuel.

My father, on the other hand, can sit for hours with a book, shifting his eyes across it while his brow stretches and shrinks. He goes from upright to sliding, from there to eased out, and lands up snoozing, the roof of the book open over his chest. He wakes up and carries on. Upright, sliding.

Books are where my father lives, where he digests and gets excited and receives his visitors. When the men from the Special Branch take him away he leaves his life behind in his books, pressed smooth and waiting to loom up from between the covers.

He smells of old trees and must, and creaks when opened. His domain is all slits and keyholes and notches of ink sunk into pages, reaching through the creamy silence of the frames.

Between the floors and the moulded-steel ceilings he ambles, from cover to cover, from shelf to shelf, making arcane jokes, wise prognostications, equations beyond dispute.

In my long grey school flannels, on tiptoe, leaning over, chin down between my knees, I keep a periodic eye on the titles. One by one I will come to know his ways, page by page, sentence by sentence; at the commas I will pause inside him. He is everywhere, waiting. One by one, I will become him.

★

64

The house is so quiet, after classes and the blunder and crunch of the rugby field. Nothing moves bar dust in the angled yellow shafts at the window; down the road, a dog. The tin roofs tremor, white-hot, the blood is still wet on the ground; backwards and they are all up, running without a sound.

★

The two men in the front seats are staring at the windscreen. Their hair is shaved to bristle, sideburns clipped. The napes of their necks come clean as a whistle out of safari-suits. My father and I are sitting behind them, holding on to each other by the eyes.

He has lost weight and looks jaded, leaning into the corner of the seat. His cheeks are flushed. He keeps his voice down low and deliberate, but everything he says is hunger.

The two men in the front seats don't flinch. Past the windscreen, heatwaves warp the bonnet of the Volkswagen.

It is my thirteenth birthday, special visit. I receive the khaki of my father's clothes, the chocolate of his corduroy jacket, the grizzled warmth of the hairs on his chest. I receive the singleness of his glance, the multitude of what he wants; the finality of his surmounted will.

I bear witness before him in the back of the Volkswagen, bring to him word of my mother his wife, my brother his son, my sister his daughter. So high, I show him with the flat of a hand. Crawls. I speak, and go numb. One clean nape twists around and announces that time is up.

My father presses my hands in his gout-studded hands. I close the car door, leaving the three of them inside. Behind me is the blunt horizon of the Fort, planted with broad-bladed aloes; in front of me, the clinic, steam shooting from a grill in the pavement. I cross the tarmac stone-cold, composing myself for my mother and a cup of tea.

The spare room: is all hush and murk. Diamond burglar-proofing hatches the shimmering plane leaves and the frilled pink petticoat flowers on the Pride of India tree. What was once a chimney now opens into long deal cupboard, with aisles of books rising up on both sides. A carved pine wardrobe squawks by the door.

The spare room has done time as a kitchen, a dining room, a bedroom, a bar. It fills up now with what no one wants and no one wants to throw away: chintz cloths and crockery from my mother's grateful patients; what's too small for me and might one day not be too big for my brother; the camel-hair coat left behind by the man who skipped the border, his leggings, his gauntlets.

The spare room is still green, from the people before. The brass lilies of its candelabra still hang from the middle of the ceiling, but no one lights them up any more. The last to do so, Mrs Scheepers, has gone, even if her lugubrious ghost lingers on.

Mrs Scheepers has a blown, seamed face, old eyes, lustreless hair pinned and cut square. She shuffles around the house in shapeless clothes under a peppermint cloud, ministering to the needs of my little sister. At all other times she is behind the spare-room door.

She is so sad, so irrevocably, hopelessly sad, her whole body must be filled with tears. The English language turns to stones in her mouth, only my sister brings any strength to her eyes. She gets no telephone calls, no letters, only the bottle-store delivery van visits her. Lieberstein's sparkling white wine occupies half the carved pine wardrobe; the top shelf is covered with Wilson's Three-X Mints, their pungent fumes waiting to be chewed out.

Mrs Scheepers is the last, my mother swears she is definitely the last and final live-in help in a slow-motion interplanetary parade through the spare room.

There is Mignonne, who likes to laze on the little crimson flowers of the Morris settee, wiggling her toes in the broken wicker-work under the far arm while doing pastels. A host of creatures move across the page in a state of pink apotheosis, coaxed on by her cooing ash-smooth jabber.

There is ratty little Mrs Taylor, and her war with the black washerwoman over singing rights in the kitchen: 'You can't,' says Mrs Taylor. And over making lunch: 'I won't,' says Mrs Taylor, confidentially adding to me that that's kaffirwork.

There is Mrs Schoeman of the high, pale cheeks protrusive as Adam's apples, deaf Mrs Schoeman whose stiff black bun turns out to be false and whose voice needs oiling. She is up with the worms, and leaves a mysterious anxiety behind when at length she retires. This is eventually pinned to the shrill tweet which comes writhing out from under her door, piercing the bones rather than the ear.

My mother knocks, discreetly at first, and calls her name. But she is asleep, with bedclothes up to her hairnet. Roused, she panics, and can't grasp what all the fuss is about. 'Fire?' she pipes in her high, rusty voice, 'Burglars?' Somewhere in the dimness we find her hearing aid, and get her to switch the shrieking off.

Mrs Schoeman has gone now, along with the rest. The new woman in our lives, Jane, is a pillar of comfort by day and, being black, out of sight in the back room at night.

The spare room is a box of shadow, smelling of Cobra polish, pressed words, a whiff of Wilson's Three-X Mints and wine from the pinewood wardrobe. Fishmoths live their vertical lives on the bookshelves; a rubbery spider enquires at the basin plughole if the tap is turned on.

The apricot tree: lifts knobbled, jointed branches over the kikuyu grass. With fissured bark, pitch on old knots and faded lichen flowers, it gives the garden a different age. The furthest twigs reach to my window, over boysenberries to the split-pole fence, to Jane's lavatory door; they brush the kennel of Chaka, the black dog, who came down to us with the house and must have peed on the tree when they were both younger, lain under it less mournfully than now in the heat of the day.

The apricot tree still manages the spring miracle, foliage. Its green stones turn into plump and honeyed and speckled purses of flesh which are duly pecked at by gangs of mousebirds, blurred by clouds of gnats and aimed at by hail unless we get there first. What falls makes delicious ammunition and is cause for spectacular skids.

Climbing the apricot tree is pie. Just so, or for its fruit, for the figs that seem reachable from its extremities but never are, for tennis balls and flying saucers stuck in the gutter. Hungry raiders are surprised slipping in to try their luck. Also up there, visiting: locusts, wasps, flies that don't buzz, brightly printed caterpillars. In permanence: weevils and worms, digesting their homes.

Shoots, twigs and sprigs are snapped off by idlers, stick fighters, grim underworld coalmen hoisting sacks of coal and pinelogs to our bins. A dancer carved by my father out of a cleft branch does the splits on the mantelpiece all the years of his absence. A giant branch is blasted by lightning, smoulders and goes grey.

Night and the apricot tree: meet with ease, the dusk sky

taking root in the deep-coloured branches. The leaves carry moonlight above the garden, making noises of water or what could be burglars or worse. Several spies have sat under them, dangling their legs into the dark air and getting a good look at our curtains.

One night Jane is out there, screaming in the shadows. 'Oh madam,' she sobs, 'he is going to kill me.' She is bleeding at the temple when let in. Her blood clots on the kikuyu grass, some sinks under.

Day and the apricot tree: meet with equal ease, the old queen's upward arms cradling blueness; what leaves she still musters rise tremoring into the breeze.

Up Oxford Road into the morning I go, buckled a little, humming some hybrid Bach. The red lion rampant on my pocket, laurel wreath in paw, waves each stone by. The load of intelligence in my canvas bag bites on one shoulder.

Up-slope I go, past jammed motor cars overheating to the flavourless tunes of Springbok Radio, past driveways winding off through leafy screens to residences concealed on high; every now and then a turret or shutter shifts between the trees.

I breathe from the broken shale rockface at my side, keeping the carbon monoxide at bay; overtake another Mercedes Benz; get overtaken by the offal man, hard at his pedals, his metal box of limp, wet, workman's lunch leaving behind a gory gleam.

At the top of the hill I pause to straighten out, strapping my swollen load to the other shoulder. The suburbs slant down to both sides under a web of greenery from which small polished motor cars emerge and start crawling upwards.

I turn left, past the shady old mansions, past the artist place upon which the Sunday papers have recently fed. People sometimes appear at its doorway with coloured stains on their clothes and electricity in their hair; they drift across the bare garden, erect and slow as ship-masts.

One morning I find a man from in there, sitting on the pavement in a deck chair, with a salty, haunted look on his face. He is surrounded by suitcases, and skeletal furniture, and a few paintings that could have been traced by fire. These are facing outwards to the road, where the motor cars inch on steadfastly muttering to themselves.

By now the red lion rampant on my pocket is nearing the walls of its destiny: here, just around the corner, comes high school. Here comes Our Father which art in heaven, Bismarck papering over the cracks, fractions and surds, bunsen burners, herds of irregular verbs. Here comes magnesium writhing in water and spitting light, lewd photographs, let me not to the marriage of true minds.

Here come the boys who will grin and bear it all: in black blazers and greys, trundling under their bags, on bicycles with playing cards beating like trapped birds against the spokes, in motor cars with their kith and kin, on Hondas and Yamahas zipping the ear up with din.

Here come the early morning tidings: the sweet triumph of Germiston Callies over the mighty Highlands Park; the mammoth struggle to dig up a certain square root, the succulence of spare ribs at the Golden Spur. Here come the diamond fists homing in unerringly on the tenderest spots along the arm; the dark jokes; the smokers, the silent ones and the minglers, the single bright collective eye that excommunicates what it cannot embrace.

Here come those who will toll all the freshest hours: Mr M of the ice-blue glance and sjambok tongue; his brother F, a pixy with a pipe and shorn white hair. 'Britannia rules the waves,' says F, ordering some unfortunate to hold out a cold palm as he raises his ruler.

Here comes Mr S, his jovial repartee working its way out of a glass-hard jowl while his eyes look us over mournfully.

Rumour has it that he once punched a man to death: now it's the Bible instead. Mr S renders perfectly the creak of a champagne bottle cork, its eruption, splutter and bubbly hush. He rails against the evils of modern advertising, especially as concerns women's underwear; and instructs us to colour all his favourite bits of Scripture, in red.

Here comes the final bell, ripping through the final book with its final intractable fact. Slack bags are fatted once again, shoulder blades sharpened as everyone stands clear of his desk. And there down below the class-rooms stretch the sportsfields, empty canvases for cramped limbs to print their violence and delight.

There goes Porfirio Bento, launching himself lithely out of gravity's lap to recline for a split instant on a sheet of air, just above the bar that marks a new high-jump record; and the crowd is on its feet, praise flaming and smoking from a thousand mouths.

The crowd is fused in a single voice, there goes Piet Cronje in a three-speed sprint skewing past the fat forwards and the flat-footed backs in their brown and yellow jerseys who get nothing but armfuls of air and grassburns in return for their efforts to crunch him down; there he goes gliding under the naked H of the rugby posts to plant the ball. And here comes the next buckling scrum all knuckles and studs, here comes the mineral taste of myself, blood, slipping from nostril to lip.

Down Oxford Road I sag into the warm aftermath of the day, steeped in fumes of wintergreen, Cornish pasty, boiled cola-rum sweets. The trees rise up to meet me, with the dumb certainty of their knowledge. I want nothing so much as a hot mothering bath.

★

The pylons: gird themselves up against the sky; like the ghosts of body-builders they lift their load of electrons and stride on pin-point legs right over the horizon. They hum as they go, the same shaky high-pitched note buzzing out of each of them, at odds with their bulky shoulders and headless necks.

They never step out of line, or turn back, or rest. If they were to congregate, there would be chaos. But the wires threaded through their struts bind them to each other all day and all night.

There are pylons in a poem that Mr E does with us in English. Over pasture, down valley and up dale they go, bringing progress to every peasant's door. Mr E explores the imagery with us in his terse, surgical way. When he stops speaking his breath drones on a bit, because of the lung he lost during the war.

The pylons in the poem are hygienic and nifty, green grass cools their feet. They don't sound like the ones at the edge of the city, whose path crosses wrinkled nicotine-stained mine-dumps, wastes of unclean stubble, oil sumps, the hulks of motor cars carrying no one halfway into the ground.

The last suburbs are hemmed in by pylons; somewhere in the distance beyond them the blacks gather, cooped up under the noxious grey flowers of their township braziers. It is a dusk country that these pylons cover with their shivering steel song, a strip of infertility, a cold frontier.

My father, according to evidence in court, was among those who blew a few of them up. In the thick of night one keels over slowly before me, flame spewing from under it, dust blinking with sparks. The other pylons stop dead in their tracks, mute and unknowing.

My father careens into the blackness with his companions, one gloved hand gripping the car wheel as he wonders what dreams will come flooding through the breach they have made.

He is gone now, and he won't be back for quite some time. But the memory of the pylon still tilts across his rear-view mirror, sinking with the terrible sweetness of a thought on fire.

★

In the maths class, Mr P explains to us about infinity: if you have a bag of marbles and want to take one out, how many times can you do this? Once. And two marbles? Twice. But how many times can you take out no marbles at all?

★

Belts: must make a dark ring of glass about the waist; toe-caps must pick sunlight from out of the dust and dazzle the eyes of the beholder. Accordingly, old polish is ironed or licked by candle-flame till it drips; last scars are scraped off with a knife. Any blade or burn mark is fatal.

The leather is shaved with glass-paper, boned smooth with a wooden block or pebble. Fresh polish is smeared on, pressed in with the back of a hot spoon, ironed through wax paper, left to dry overnight. It is then rubbed up, compounded with spittle, disk by overlapping silvery disk, each a little wider than the tip of the forefinger which is going stiff behind its rag.

By now the belt is in some sheltered place where no ignorant hand will flap it up and down; it might be safely buckled around a cake-tin. The boots are buried somewhere. Any sign of crackling in the gloss brings on panic and the urge to begin again.

This urge is sometimes collective and usually occurs at the last minute, in which case circles of polishers sit rubbing and spitting into the small hours. Those who are desperate or unscrupulous turn to other means: lemon, egg-white, vinegar, hair-lacquer and wood varnish have all been risked, bringing on various degrees of disaster.

Meanwhile flashes must be sewn onto shoulders, brasswork buffed, puttees creamed, khaki shorts and shirt pressed. The beret badge must be screwed to something firm and invisible, a sprung wire spiffy engineered so that the collar does not jump to the chin in the middle of proceedings. Garters must be improvised, to prevent the shame of socks falling to half-mast. Queues form daily at the armoury for what's gone missing or has been mutilated beyond repair.

On the morning of the competition, Trojans, Spartans, Romans, Thebans and Tuscans converge on the school grounds earlier than usual. Some bear their uniforms aloft on hangers, belts still round cake-tins, boots in a bag. Others, already in full dress, displace themselves gingerly, erect, will not sit or bend, stick to the tarmac or flagstones and keep away from grass or sand like the plague. Many have thick eyelids and pink eyeballs. Paleness at the nape of the neck and behind the ears betrays where the barber has been.

Everyone forms up in platoons. Those about to bark, expectorate behind clean handkerchiefs. Those about to obey check what glints or does not on their neighbours, glance up at the strong climbing sun and hope it does not strike them down. There follows an endlessness of barking and obeying in which only the sickly, the odds and the sods do not participate.

Someone barks best and gets the Sword of Honour. Spartans obey best, or Thebans, or whichever, and get indulgent smiles from the masters in charge. It has taken a year of Thursdays to come to this, and it will take a year of Thursdays to come to it again. Manhood is just around the bend.

★

Michelle's hair-do: is not quite what I bargained for, but I concentrate all my attention on the crazy paving as I escort her to the car. Inside, half-sunk into the upholstery, I don't touch Michelle over-much; tingle where I do. The others make cool laughter as the matric dance comes looming ineluctably through the dark.

Amidst a rustling of skirts and a smoothing of suits, we are delivered into the spotlights of the school-hall patio. Many others are already seated around the milk-white table-cloths, in a glaze of Brylcream and satin, banter and blush. Light catches on cuff-links, spangles, the little silvered pinheads tugging the collar against the knot of the tie. Eyes hover around us as we arrive; soon they will no doubt be zooming in on the promontory of Michelle's hair-do.

Michelle's hair-do is balanced on her head in tapering lacquered tiers, brown and sticky and smelling of insect repellent. I have never seen it there before, and can find no connection between it and the girl I wanted so badly to take to the dance.

Michelle, however, seems comfortable enough just the way she is, sitting next to me with her clear skin mummified under some pinkish lotion and her shy lips reddened in; when she opens them they look as if they have floated through the air from her upside-down cone of hair.

After a lot of big pauses and small talk, Michelle and I negotiate the sound-waves in the hall, the mass of flapping elbows that shifts weight from one leg to the next. It is not long before we are washed outside again, on to firm brick in the breeze, sweetening our mouths with drink.

We have hardly edged in for a second attempt when the rhythm eases up and everyone is suddenly divided into twos, cheek to jowl and shoe to shoe. We just slow down our elbows, and drag our feet. Gradually in the blue gloom we drift apart, until I entirely lose sight of the tip of Michelle's hair-do.

I drift in the pulsating air, out of step, with no alibi for being there; such a blur of rocked bodies where the morning before we had mouthed Our Father which art in heaven, such altered skins for this twisting ceremony. A girl in cellophane gathers a swarm of light against her as she is swirled by her partner. He sports a young moustache that was kept hidden under a Band-Aid all week.

Around them are others of my elasticated schoolmates, school faces lost in dance. And between swags of streamers on the walls are photographs of the cream of many crops, arms and ankles folded, grinning out across a dimness of years.

Then Michelle's hair-do is back and I can't find any words to bring her out from underneath it. Fortunately the hour is getting late, cars are pulling up at the gate. I am squeezed against Michelle once more. She tells me not to bother about walking her to the door.

What puzzles me is that the next time we meet, she seems as fresh and unfancy as the girl I had wanted to be with on the dance floor.

Tretchikoff's rose: stands in a see-through glass vase with a slender neck. Thorns prick into the water, bubbles suck at the stalk. The petals of Tretchikoff's rose are roused to yearning, ready with dew; at the calyx a few blouse out. One has fallen to the table-top, where it lies vaguely reflecting itself next to a dew-drop encased in light. Behind the rose a curtain of gloom absorbs all heat and lends cold fervour to the redness of the petals.

The rose hangs from the wall in Mike's room, looking out past the S-bends of the electric racing-car circuit through a first-floor window to the garden where its progenitors perfume their beds. The tennis court is fenced off to the right, perfectly rolled and freshly quartered with white lines. The swimming-pool cuts a rippling blue oval in the crazy paving, hemmed in by the crispness of kikuyu grass.

Mike and I get into tennis togs under the rose, then follow the florid passage-carpet down the stairs. At the bottom, an iron gate is swung back into the stairwell. In the reception rooms, sun-rays through lace are caught on chair arms and china, sunk in pile.

After the game, tea steaming on a silver tray, or syrupy coloured fizz, as our whim might be, is borne into the breakfast room by white-jacketed Jonas. Mike complains about a stain on the table-cloth and Jonas spreads a fresh one with a smile.

Upstairs, then. Stretched through ease to torpor, judging and jibing at each other, we slowly change. It will take me as long to reach home now as a slug. Hung to the wall, Tretchikoff's rose bears witness, from out of the cold oils of its flesh.

Game: most of us go disguised into the city streets, the rest must pick us out. Rules, for us: stick to four designated blocks, don't go indoors. Ignore strangers. Act normal. Fade into the scenery. If someone can whisper your name in your ear, change out of your costume and join the rest. Rules for the rest: keep your eyes skinned.

Soon we are all found out: the round lady with two pillows under his dress, the French artiste with a scratchy charcoal moustache, those who decide to go and have steakburgers instead. The blind man finds himself doing a real blind man's beat. The three tarts in leather jackets get themselves found by their sweethearts.

We meet at Fontana bakery at the appointed time, buy ourselves cassata icecreams, and stand out in the sunlight of the plaza chewing through cold cherries. Someone decides to take a count, and then, in consternation, a re-count. He is three short.

Mystery: whatever happened to Michael and Maurice and Johnny? We return to the four blocks, split up, and comb the population. We look too eagerly at a few offended strangers, come up with nothing and make a worried knot as we compile a list of telephone numbers: parents, police if necessary.

Right next to us, the three blacks who have been sitting all this while against a wall, finally stand up. They are wearing blue overalls, old tackies. They take off their battered straw hats.

IV Watched

On the tar apron: we stand and wait. Daylight shrivels into stars, deserting our suitcases and heads shorn bald as fists. Trucks everywhere saw up the darkness. Anyone who thinks he can talk or turn will get his block knocked off.

In a shed: there are two slabs of Atlas bread each, along with some gluey soup. There is also a gap in a roneoed letter which smells fresher than the bread. The gap must be filled with a number; number's family can then be informed that it, number, is not yet dead.

In another shed, the next day, the marriage ceremony is held. First, we are loaded with the dowry: greatcoat, underclothes, ground sheet, braces, belt, helmet, water-bottle, jerkin, shirts and so on, seventy items lovingly counted out and placed in our open arms by someone whose face the rising pile fortunately obliterates. Next, a rifle is balanced on the pile by a row of thick knuckles. It is announced that this rifle is my wife, and that the penalty will be divorce and worse if she should be dropped. Bursts of laughter end the ceremony.

On the tar apron: we stand and wait. It is after the ceremony. We are dressed for the Pole, to lessen the load which must now be borne to the nuptial bed. Sweat washes over us. The sun is a diamond revolving in a pure blue hand. We are ordered to return to our bungalows and lurch forward, trailing braces, boots, hems, hugging our wives.

The bungalow: is for inspection, and most especially the beds. The bedclothes must be bound to the mattress, and flattened with the back of a mess tin. The pillow must never show any sign of its head. Zealots in fact sleep under their beds. Before dawn we have to climb the walls to get to the windows, and rub until we see bits of our bleary selves in the glass and the brass.

Corporal Pretorius: is not for laughing at, an earnest minion whose face has few movable parts. 'Listen, you got problems with pimples? Shave them off man, shave them off.' According to Corporal Pretorius, the bungalow is for running around if you can't get washed before you've woken up.

The scream: is pumped out by a row of lungs on the run. It must come, now, above the boots in their red cloud, as the bayonet seeks the heart marked on the ground. The scream rips out with a life of its own, blood-streaked, eyes creased shut. It will help death to find a home.

★

I enter the hut in the old mine compound. Soldiers are speeding through the glare outside, dodging doors and windows and sticking to walls. Boots crunch up the gravel, dust flies. A window is cracked open by mistake and an officer yelps as if his tail had been stood on.

The hut is cool and sombre. Bunks in cramped tiers of three on either side are separated by no more than the length of a rifle. Near the one dirt-crusted, burglar-proofed window stands a coal stove, the ghosts of callused miners' hands hovering over it.

Pasted on the mud walls to face the heads of sleeping miners are pictures torn from glossy magazine ads: a trim gold lighter, a string of pearls glowing around a swan-white neck, a wrist-watch bursting with rays of light.

Boots come thudding around the hut, there is panting at the door. I put my helmet back on my damp head and run out, doubled up, rifle ready for the enemy.

I want to be arrested so that I can read the Bible. Everyone is being arrested, or receiving special visits in the middle of his dreams, or hearing trees shake when there isn't even a breeze. One might at least expect to walk outside in the morning and find the rosebushes with their toes up in the air, freshly dug holes in the ground around them where someone was prospecting for banned books. But ever since they came for my father, our house has been unfairly ignored.

Once again I begin the Book of Genesis. Once again the light is divided from darkness, the waters under the heavens are gathered together unto one place and the dry land appears. But there is always some interruption. I have to drive off to the Greek café to buy some cat-food, or fetch my brother from judo, or the newspaper lands on the lawn covered in blood.

I unfold it, and out fall foaming dog-bites and well-sharpened bicycle spokes, hose-pipes fixed from gas-taps to lovers' mouths, black widow spiders, boxing gloves and bars of soap. Out fall laws and words of the dead. By the middle of the night the grass is still red.

But the house is so quiet. My brother and sister have sunk into sleep. My mother is learning about nerve-messages and electricity. Nyanga the schizophrenic cat is up a tree, stalking moonlight. The house is so quiet, standing in its garden in the night. There are only the termites picking at its foundations, and then my mother running a bath.

Suddenly there is a rash of car doors slamming all around our block and I think to myself this is it, they are coming to take me away. I hold my breath waiting for our gate to squeak open, wondering how I am going to get at my toothbrush now that my mother has locked herself into the bathroom. But then the cars grunt and rumble off, there must have been another meeting at the Cripple School across the road.

I want to be arrested so that I can read the Bible, right through from the beginning to the end. I have had enough of this suspension in the cool jasmine air, neither here nor there, the blacks and the others surrounding me with their ancestral bones and their battles, staking out a birthright which is not mine.

I want four pocked walls and a little lock in the door, steps going in the other direction down the corridor. And then at last I will open the Book, and set out across its fine-beaten burning words.

I will learn their ancient shivering heat, the way they heap and flex and infinitely divide. Facet by facet I will follow the contours of their questioning.

And at night I will watch the darkness cover them, letter by letter claiming their white territory, until they each subside and go dumb. And in their silent company I will lay myself down, flat and faithful as a bookmark, waiting for daylight to deliver the next sentence.

★

I wake up feeling sombre and sealed in like a bomb. The day stands outside tall and blue, with dogs at its feet and light bursting from its head.

According to the news, Charlie Brown and Snoopy were up into the early hours in a pumpkin patch, anxiously awaiting the coming of the Big Pumpkin. Meanwhile, Peter Magubane spent his 566th night in detention without trial. The prisons are packed, and owing to lack of space people have been waking up to find their own houses fitted out with judas, bars, bugs and guardian.

But our house has, apparently, once again been ignored. I blink my way into the garden, looking for tracks in the flower beds, boots under the hedge. Nothing. The rosebushes are in the pink of health. There is no one pretending to be a newspaper in a Volkswagen down the road.

On campus, students are sprawled out across the library lawn between piles of books, studying other students. There are small interruptions for lectures and then more studying, which culminates in heated discussions as to who is definitely a spy and who only might be.

After lunch there are all the picket lines toeing the pavement down one side of the campus. We have to stand off the pavement and we have to stand still, so that those who wish to can perform the difficult task of mixing us into a batter of raw eggs and flour from a moving car. They also manage to add in a few sweet words for good measure.

One afternoon there is the march to John Vorster Square. It is just an ordinary afternoon in Johannesburg. Bus-conductors, tea-boys, schoolgirls, three-piece businessmen, dentists with hygienic mouths, messengers, steak-house waiters, airplane-glue sniffers and secretaries pass through the giant shadows in their uniforms. Up in the sky, men hang from

90

platforms polishing walls of mirrors.

Traffic cops stop the traffic for us, passers-by wave or gape or politely turn their backs, pigeons flap off. Signs invite us to buy Stern's diamonds and All Gold jams, one urges us to attend ballroom dancing classes.

In a cloud of chants stuck with placards and a banner marked 'Charge or Release' we roll on to the west end of town. The broken white line slips under our feet. I am holding the hand of a girl with sea-green eyes and a fugitive smile whose flashing I would like to cover with my lips.

The police appear with muscles bulging out of clean slate safari suits, combs in the socks that reach up to their knee-caps and truncheons in their fists. Behind them rises the implacable anthem-blue façade of John Vorster Square, framed in silver. They collect our placards at the door and let us in.

We are locked into an inner courtyard where we stand flushed and shivering, 357 of us. One girl works herself into a red frenzy and faints. Corridors full of footsteps lengthen around us. A tin is lowered at the end of some string from a barred window above our heads, with a note in it saying, 'Hello, got any smokes?' The day fades and we are still there, making unlikely plans and nervous jokes. A police officer comes and interrupts us. It is time to go home, he says. At the door they roll ink onto our hands and flash bulbs in our faces. We step out into the evening air. Back home, there is mutton stew and fruit salad for supper.

★

The campus blacks: wear sunglasses, or look shifty, or plant a glance of acid in the eyes of those who seek them out. They often stand alone, looking glum and hungry for the unnameable matter that is fattening the minds of the whites all around them. They hold books and note-pads in their hands, but rarely attend lectures in the arts courses for which they cannot register.

No one knows quite what to do about them. They find a way into the discussion groups on the library lawn, and sit there like the hidden, hairy root of the problem while flowery words sprout out of everyone else's mouth. They arrive at parties where they sip liquor all evening, and have to be driven miles out into the chilly smogbound no man's land of the townships in the early hours.

No one knows quite what they live on, or where they get their tasteful new clothes. They have no kinship with the white-coated technicians or the cleaners in blue, nothing at all to do with the dull khaki bulks of night-watchmen bent over their trusty knobkerries waiting for burglars, or a flight of right-winged pamphleteers, or anyone who might again try to paint across the campus walls such homilies as 'Halitosis is the last line of defence.'

The campus blacks don't fade into anonymity, nor do they fit anywhere else. They look on as the whites collect in a hot and jagged mass under a banner marked 'Remember Sharpeville,' and drag it down, and cause it to die a serpent's death, stamping on it until little stones stick through. They are on their way out by the time the picket lines form down Jan Smuts Avenue.

The campus blacks disappear, one by one. It is rumoured that some have been detained; then a few of them are back again, looking haunted and hinting at police brutality. If they had been spies, why were they brutalised? If they hadn't been, why are they free? Perhaps they weren't, but have assumed a new identity?

They continue to stand alone with their books and their hunger, under the chestnut tree, against the wooden huts. But they move even more cautiously now, stiltwalking step by step through the dire discussions and the cool suburban fun.

★

The pulsing: comes over the vulvar shimmering of rock flowers, through the heat that snakes off parked cars. Shudder after shudder deep sound-waves heave up, engulfing the coo of lovers on the lawn, juicy squeals from the swimming-pool.

Chair legs jiggle upside-down on tables in the Student Union canteen, the green lino floor shakes over and over; what chugging flood raises the foundations through a blue Saturday afternoon?

They crowd in the Women's Common Room up above. Some sit on long tables against the walls, shoulder to silvered black shoulder, stripped to the waist, clapping. Others stand and stamp soles flat, slaps shocking the floor. All gazes are drawn to the dancers, their backs angled, buttocks up, knees nocked to chest and unleashed between horn-stiff arms as

93

they punctuate their pride into the beat, mating through the throb.

There is nothing in the room to hold onto, books on the shelves can't keep still. The whole place rocks up and down on the way back to Africa.

Wind beats grass pale copper, beyond the wastes it undulates and sweeps alive the bottom of the sky. And against hips grass, sweet stem, sour stem she takes me down; slack wires pulled to a smile for passage, blackjack, burr, spindrift of something's bubbles, islands of dung burning with blowflies, dry waters of grass sounding with the drone.

The ground dips, going bald. Walls forget themselves brick by brick; sticks half melted to ash, cracked bones are still warm with conversation. The bow-legged beetle in his stirrups, the pied bug up-blade, under-blade walk where my want is; the snuff tin lies there, the limp-snouted condom, the little crinkle-eyed milkweed seed riding its puff of whiteness.

Where the grass masses again, its rustling supple resistance grown on the upslope, in the black arms of the firebreak she turns, compact and chthonic and terse, and turns me in the restless autumn of her hair, the inner laughing green of her glance.

Grass billows back behind us through the afternoon, laps at hedgerow and pine-needle bed, maroon field seamed with the flaming thread of flowers. In the garden, grass knots low around shrub and herb and tree, under the blue alcohol of the wisteria, up to bamboo rods tugging at the sky and things wriggling in the pool that usually fly.

Thatched grass slants comfortably grey over the house, raises a few eyebrows thickly at the upper windows, rests on the broad old spirit of the beams. Its smoky odour meets with lavender, beeswax and udder-warm cream in the ample, drowsy roundness of the rooms; it permeates her family's loving and feuding. Even the servants must slow their pace to navigate the dense currents.

She takes me in, telling secrets about the carob bean and the orgies of the bee. She sits me down and stirs a brew of lemon, sage and bluegum honey. I drink it in a dream, and in a dream wander over the sliced-stone floors, through polished doorways, past her enticing sisters one by one.

I return to her with the blinking eyes of a stranger who has just learned of the possibility that he comes from nowhere else. Married to your mother she says, helping me to unbutton her blouse.

She lays my body out between the charred blunt stubble and the sun, seals my eyes shut with her tongue; then fetches dressfuls of freshly scythed grass to pour over me, all the while singing those tone-deaf songs she knows.

I am a pulse of sap and cellulose. Threads of hot oxygen end at my nostrils. Sweat washes and stings me, lacewing and ant investigate fretfully. Her songs lighten and the tides of grass lift them away. I lie still on the firebreak, in a long flickering procession between absence and waking.

The span of the journey

The further back we go, the greater will be the span of the journey to come. Eventually, we will reach a place no larger than the last footprint of a swimmer entering the sea.

The further back we go, the more certain were some people of our coming.

Why do our memories appear only as the backwash of the wave? Does the sea have only a single shore?

The three days after his release, my father spends in front of the bookshelves; three days is all he has. He kneels down on all fours, stretches up tall with his arms above his head, climbs to mid-air in a cloud of dust.

At nightfall he is still there, with books crowded below him on the floor, books hanging over the edges of crates, and many more in a state of collapse on the shelves.

Everyone else falls asleep, but my father can't sleep; he pauses at a doorway listening to the deep breaths, shaking his head in disbelief, wandering on to the next doorway with the unsure step of a passenger going down a gangplank onto dry land.

By the third night my father has packed up all the walls, book by book, and sent them off by boat so that the family will have a place to stay in the next country it gets to.

On the third night the garden enters my sleep, a mottled wilderness, migrant country, with no frontiers, all houses sunk behind foliage and shadow. And everywhere there are men on the move, such numbers of them that the ground itself seems to be shifting.

There are men with empty suitcases and shapeless coats, men with candles waxed to their hats and moths glittering around them, men reclining for a while in garden beds with pay-day scars on their faces and a bottle of white lightning in an inside pocket, men bending this way and that over the earth as if gifted with the cleft mind of the divining rod.

Under a pear tree stands my mother, watching them as they

drift past. Her flashing eyes light up the proud lines of her face, but the men don't seem to notice her. She stands there, whispering to herself: 'I am a burnt page, I am a burnt page, blow on me and I will scatter.' And then the sounds go out, slowly she turns, and the garden is in blackness.

MORE CARCANET FICTION

Sebastian Barry   *The Engine of Owl-Light*
'He must be regarded as one of the most promising of our writers, displaying a technical ambition and an emotional maturity . . .'
IRISH TIMES

Emmanuel Bove   *Armand*
'. . . does for Paris what Ulysses did for Dublin.'   THE NEW YORKER

Christine Brooke-Rose   *Xorandor*
'. . . verbal pyrotechnics are deployed in the interest of heightening and enriching her story, which is always riveting.'
NEW YORK TIMES BOOK REVIEW

Dino Buzzati   *The Tartar Steppe*
'It is not often a masterpiece falls into one's hand . . . *The Tartar Steppe* is a sublime book and Buzzati a master of the written word.'   SUNDAY TIMES

Stuart Hood   *A Storm from Paradise*
'. . . its passionate artistic truth is conveyed in writing so plain, realistic and indeed functionally beautiful that one learns its sad lessons from history with joy.'   FINANCIAL TIMES

Clarice Lispector   *The Hour of the Star*
'The literary discovery of the decade'   VOGUE

Pier Paolo Pasolini   *A Violent Life* and *The Ragazzi*
'. . . both are extraordinary. Written in the 1950s, they are energetic, blithely amoral accounts of life in the suburban slums of Rome, seen largely through the eyes of their more or less criminal inhabitants.'   THE LISTENER

Umberto Saba   *Ernesto*
'This little gem is the last testament of one of Italy's most revered modern poets. A lovely, classical portrait of adolescence.'
BOOKLIST (ALA)

Leonardo Sciascia   *Sicilian Uncles* and *One Way or Another*
'What is the Mafia mentality? What is the Mafia? What is Sicily? When it comes to the exploration of this particular hell, Leonardo Sciascia is the perfect Virgil.'   GORE VIDAL

Michael Westlake   *Imaginary Women*
A novel to be read as geopolitics, as postmodernism, as homage to Hollywood, as psychoanalysis, as anarchic fiction . . .